PIANO · VOCAL · GUITAR

CASTING CROWNS

ISBN 0-634-08037-7

HAL·LEONARD®
CORPORATION
7777 W. BLUEMOUND RD. P.O. BOX 13819 MILWAUKEE, WI 53213

Visit Hal Leonard Online at
www.halleonard.com

CONTENTS

WHAT IF HIS PEOPLE PRAYED

Words and Music by MARK HALL
and STEVEN CURTIS CHAPMAN

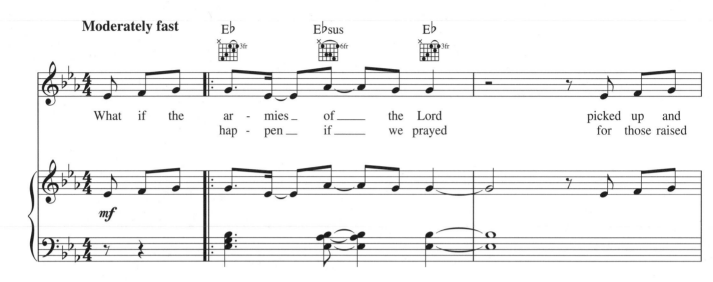

What if the ar - mies_ of ___ the Lord picked up and
hap - pen ___ if ___ we prayed for those raised

dust - ed ___ off ___ their swords, vowed to
up to ___ lead ___ the way? Then may - be

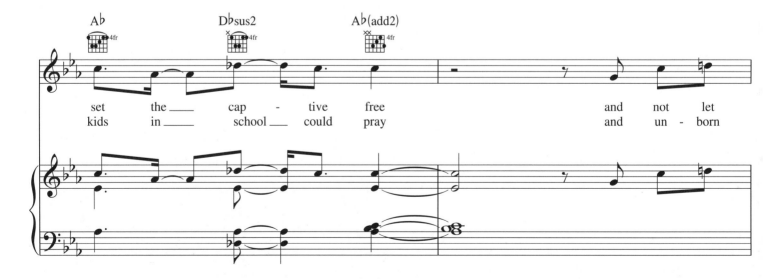

set the ___ cap - tive free and not let
kids in ___ school ___ could free pray and un - born

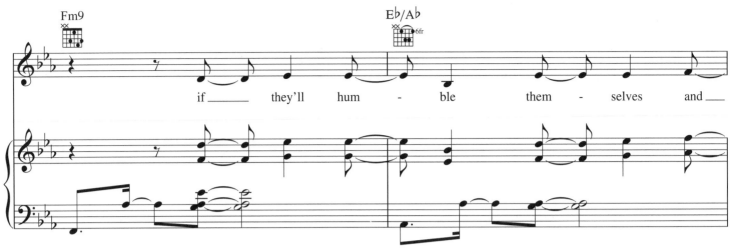

if _____ they'll hum - ble them - selves and _____

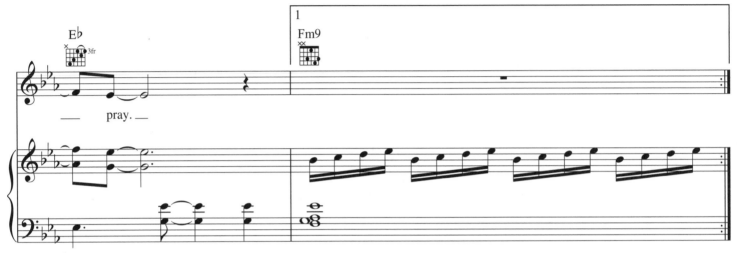

_____ pray. _____

Male: What if His peo - ple prayed, _____

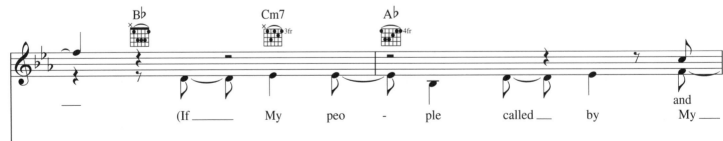

(If _____ My peo - ple called _____ by My _____ and

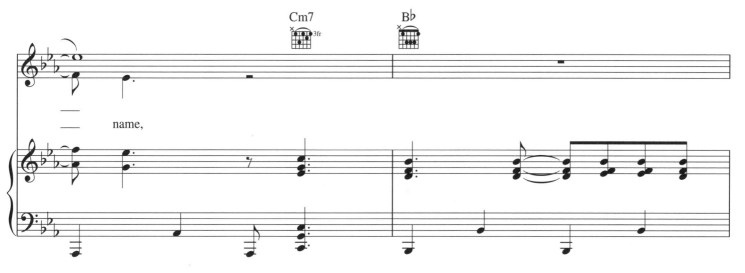

name,

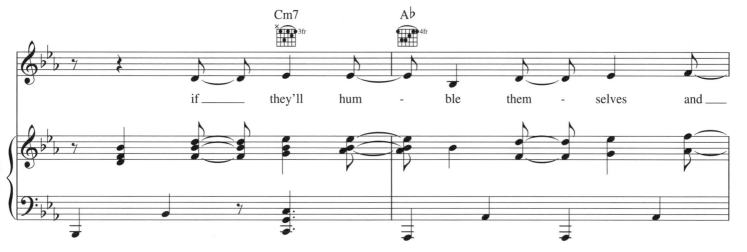

if _____ they'll hum - ble them - selves and ____

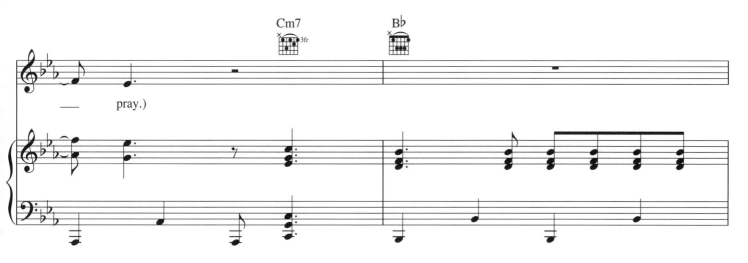

__ pray.)

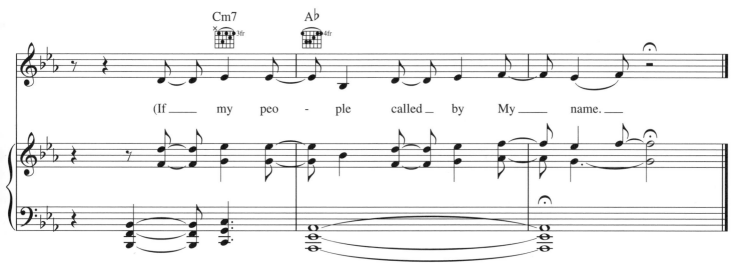

(If ____ my peo - ple called __ by My ____ name. ____

IF WE ARE THE BODY

Words and Music by
MARK HALL

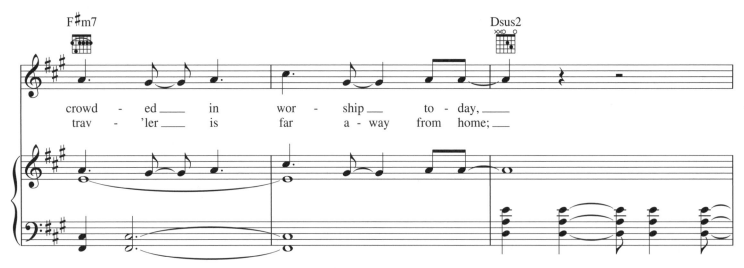

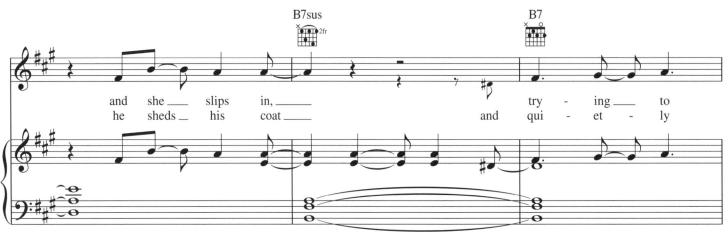

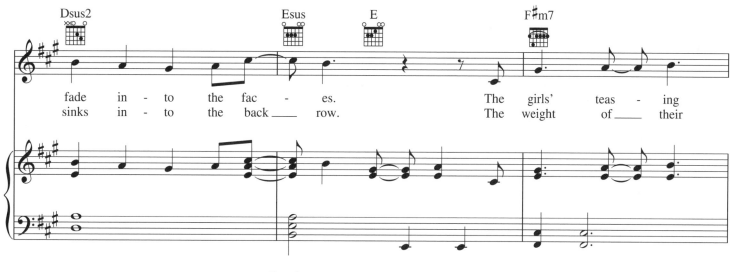

fade in - to the fac - es. The girls' teas - ing
sinks in - to the back row. The weight of their

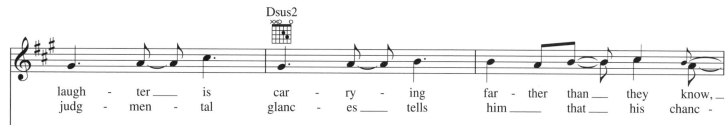

laugh - ter is car - ry - ing far - ther than they know,
judg - men - tal glanc - es tells him that his chanc -

- es are bet - ter out on the road.

far - ther than they know.

But if we are the bod - y, why aren't His arms

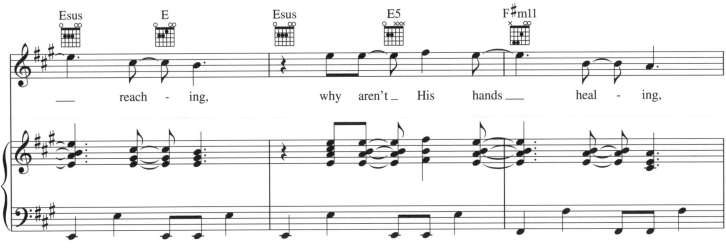

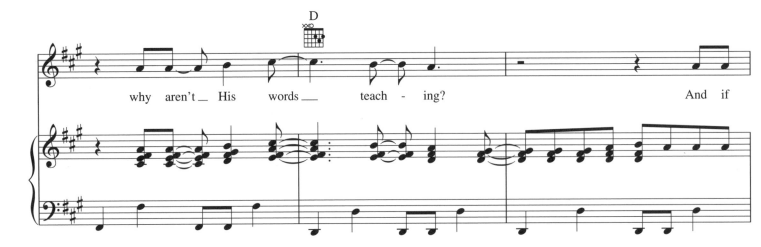

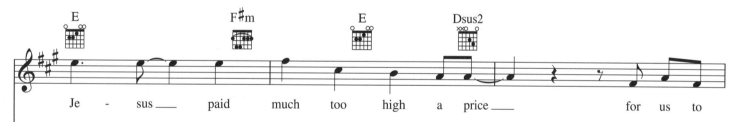

If we are the bod - y,

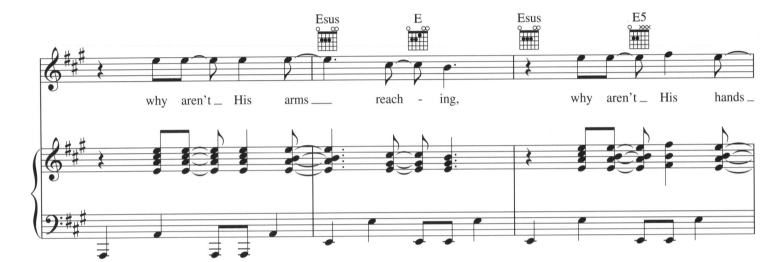

why aren't __ His arms __ reach - ing, why aren't __ His hands __

__ heal - ing, why aren't __ His words __ teach - ing?

And if we are the bod - y, why aren't __ His feet __

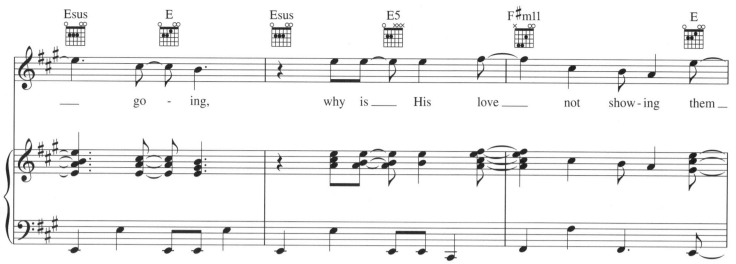

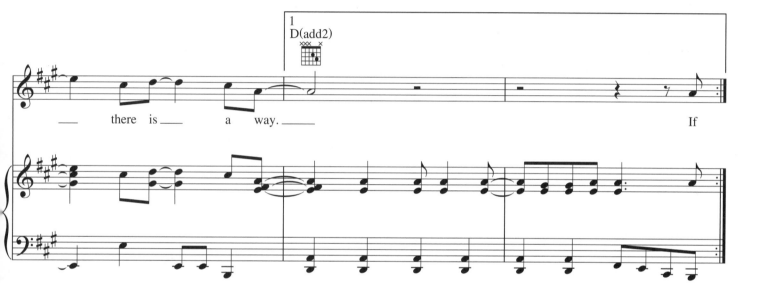

VOICE OF TRUTH

Words and Music by MARK HALL
and STEVEN CURTIS CHAPMAN

Moderately slow

Oh what I _____ would do _____ to have _____ the kind of faith _____ it takes _____ to climb out _____ of this boat I'm in, _____

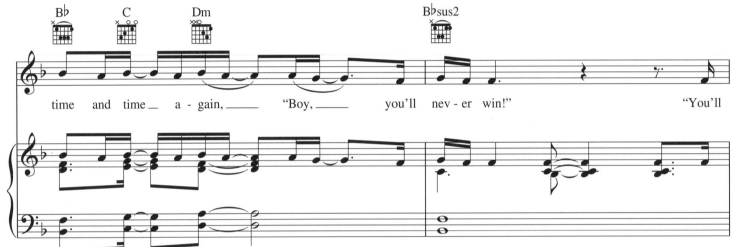

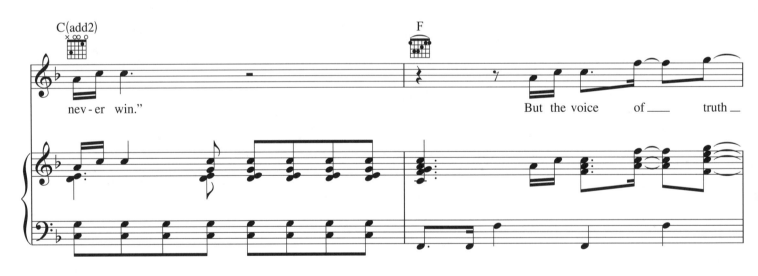

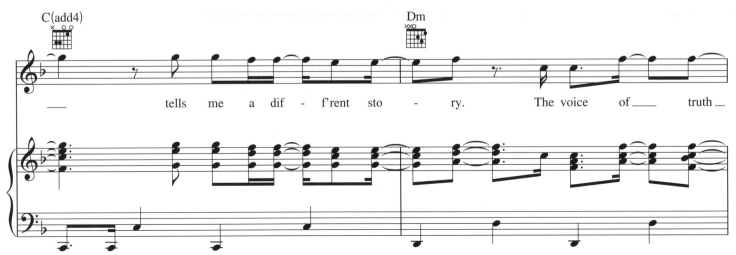

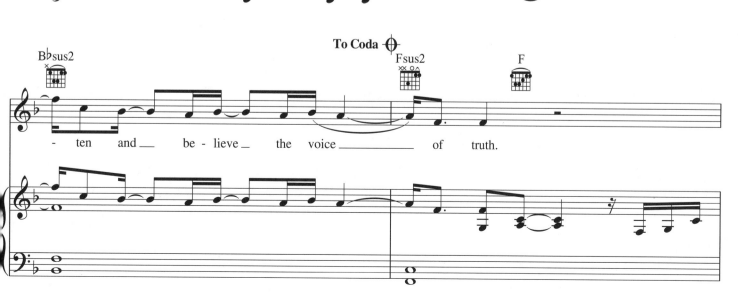

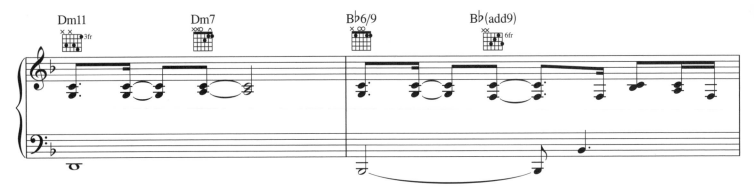

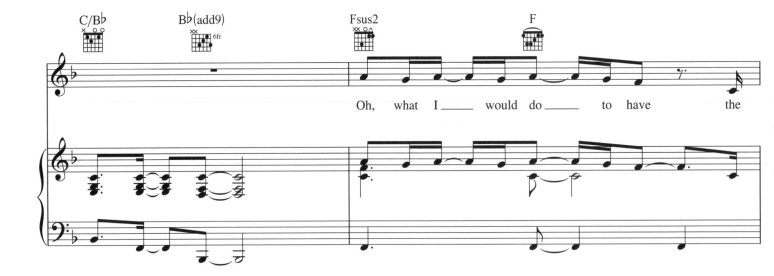

Oh, what I ____ would do _____ to have ____ the

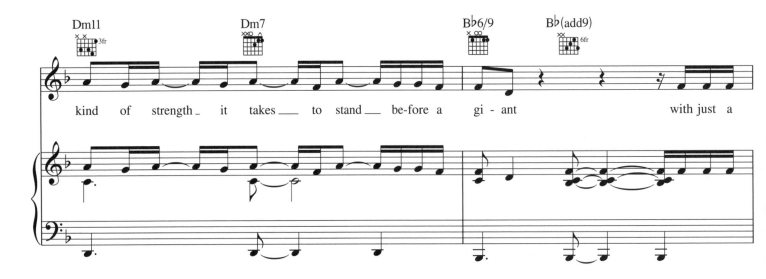

kind of strength __ it takes ____ to stand ____ be-fore a gi - ant with just a

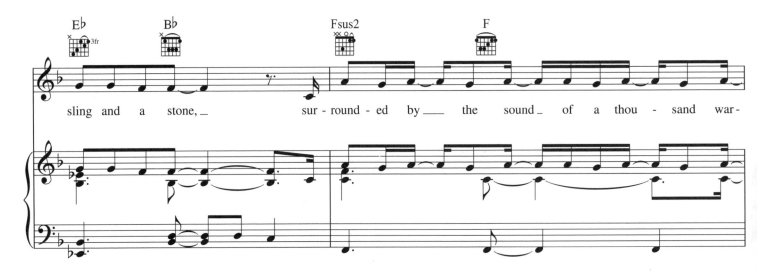

sling and a stone, ____ sur - round - ed by ____ the sound __ of a thou - sand war-

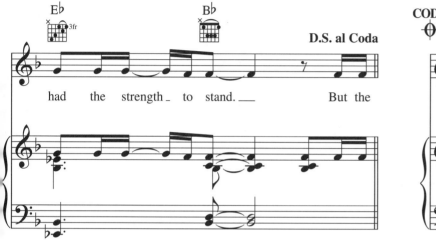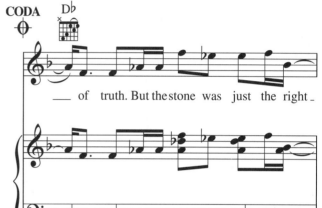

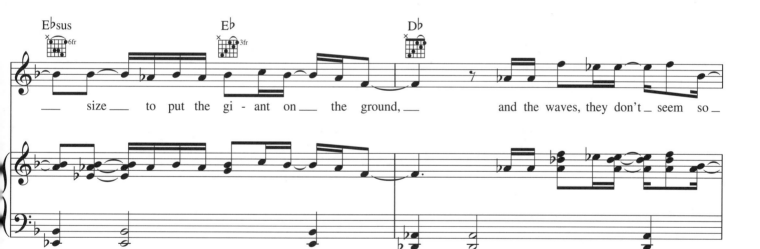

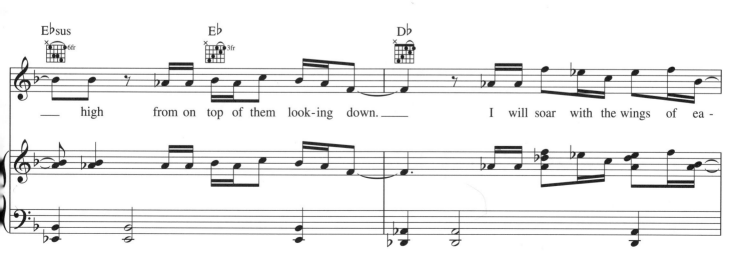

-gles when I stop __ and lis - ten to __ the sound __ of Je - sus

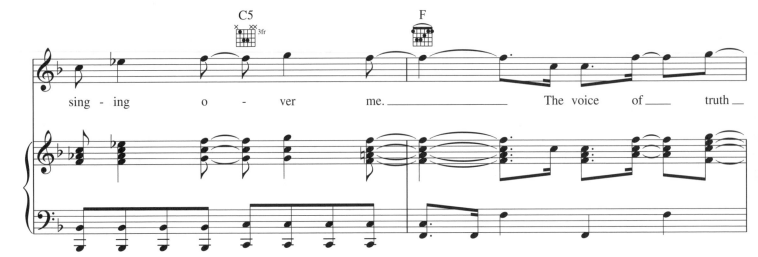

sing - ing o - ver me. _____ The voice of __ truth __

__ tells me a dif - f'rent sto - ry. The voice of __ truth __

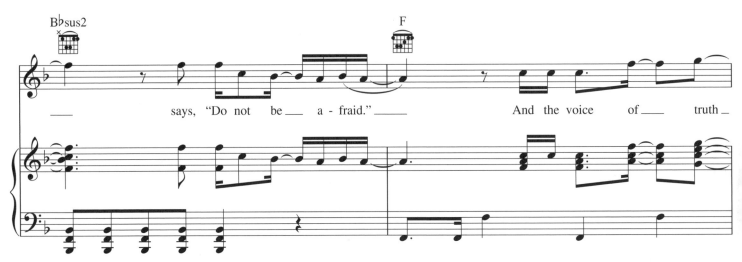

__ says, "Do not be __ a - fraid." ____ And the voice of __ truth __

says, "This is for My glo - ry." Out of all the voic - es

call - ing out to me, I will choose to lis -

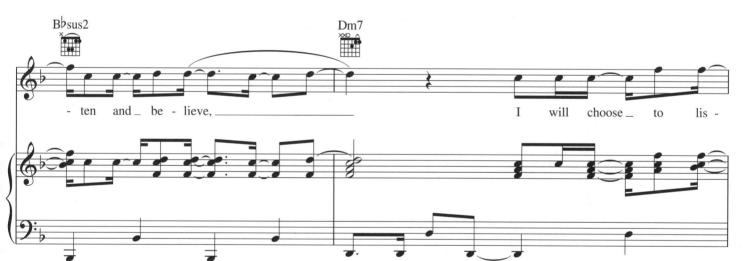

- ten and be - lieve, I will choose to lis -

- ten and be - lieve the voice

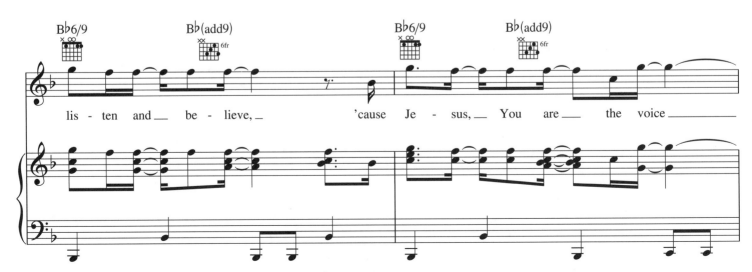

of truth, _____ and I will

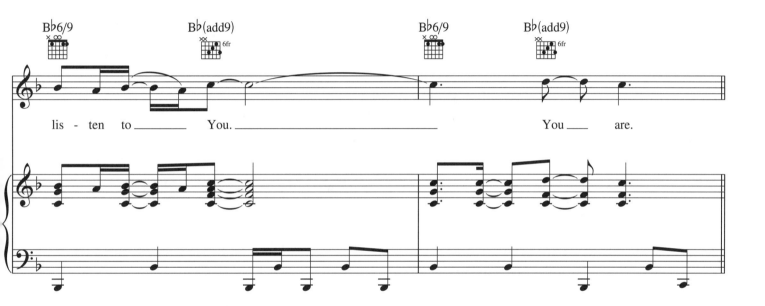

lis - ten to _____ You._____ You ___ are.

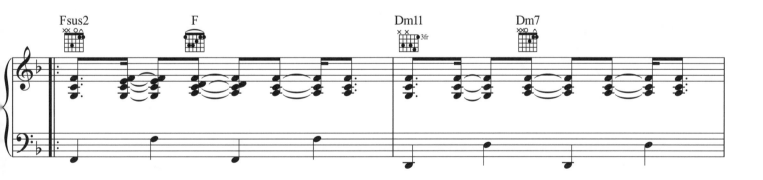

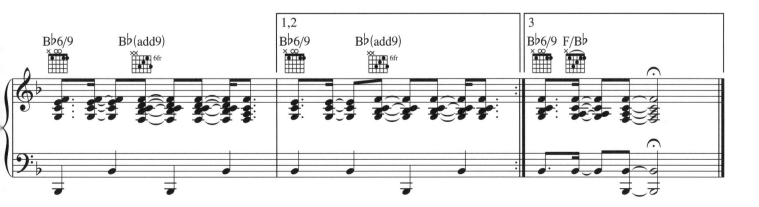

WHO AM I

Words and Music by
MARK HALL

* *Recorded a half step higher.*

cause of what __ You've done. __ Not be - cause of what __ I've done, __

__ but be - cause of who __ You are, _____

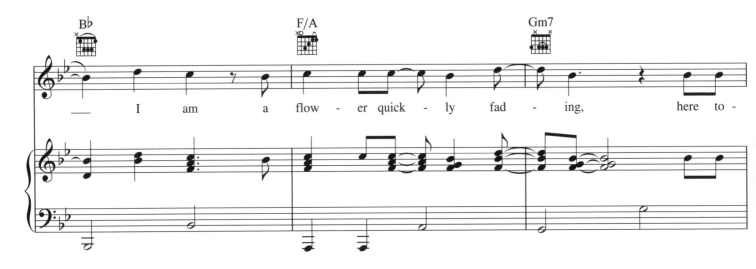

__ I am a flow - er quick - ly fad - ing, here to -

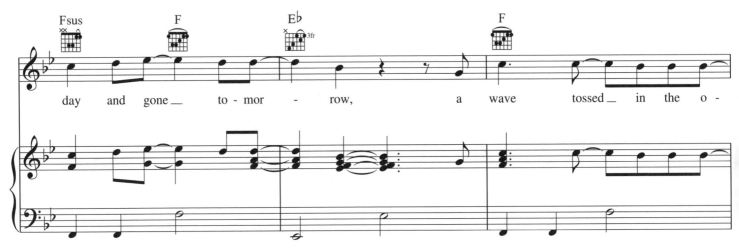

day and gone __ to - mor - row, a wave tossed __ in the o -

-cean, a va-por in ___ the wind. ___ Still You

hear me when ___ I'm call - ing. Lord, You catch me when ___ I'm fall -

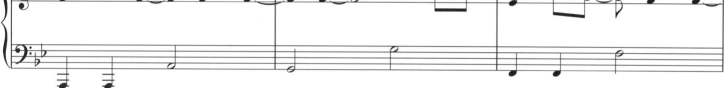

To Coda ⊕

-ing and You've told me who ___ I am: ___

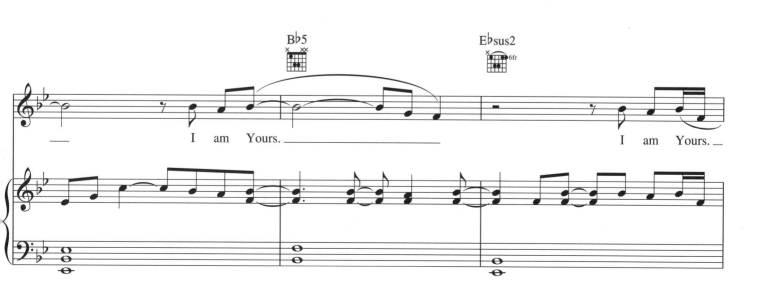

I am Yours. ___ I am Yours. ___

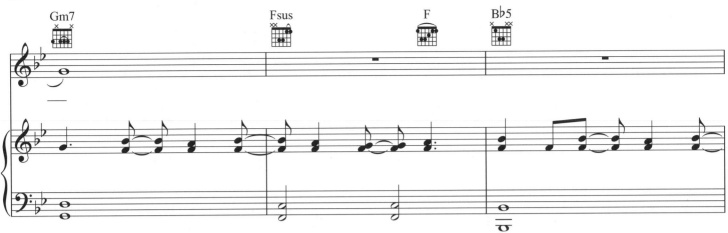

Who am I

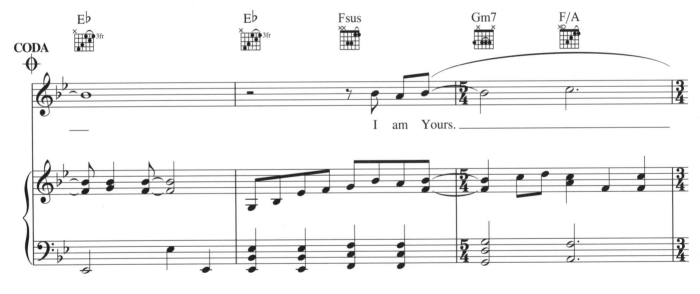

CODA

I am Yours.

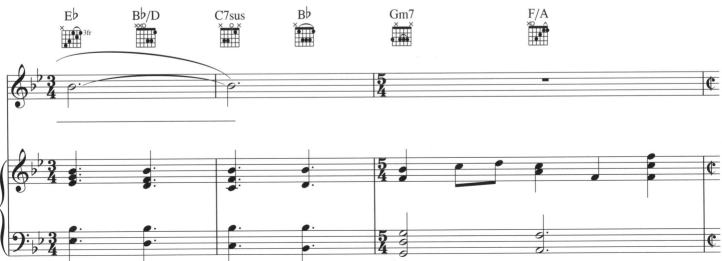

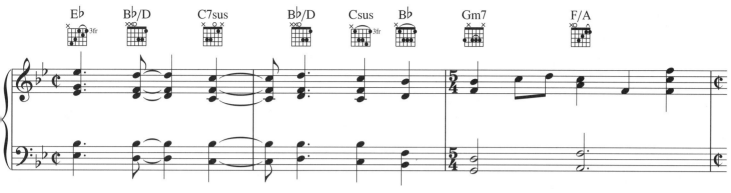

Not be - cause of who __ I am, ___ but be -

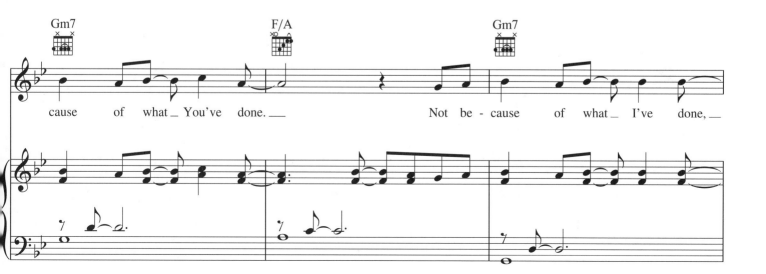

cause of what __ You've done. ___ Not be - cause of what __ I've done, __

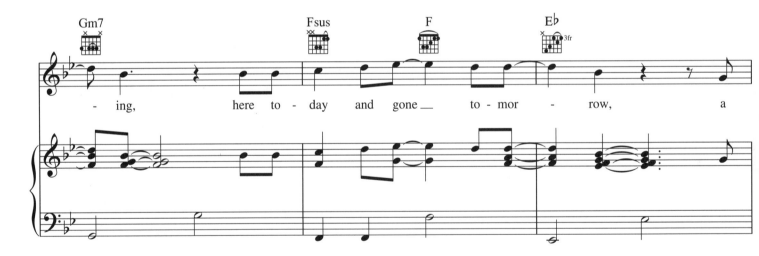

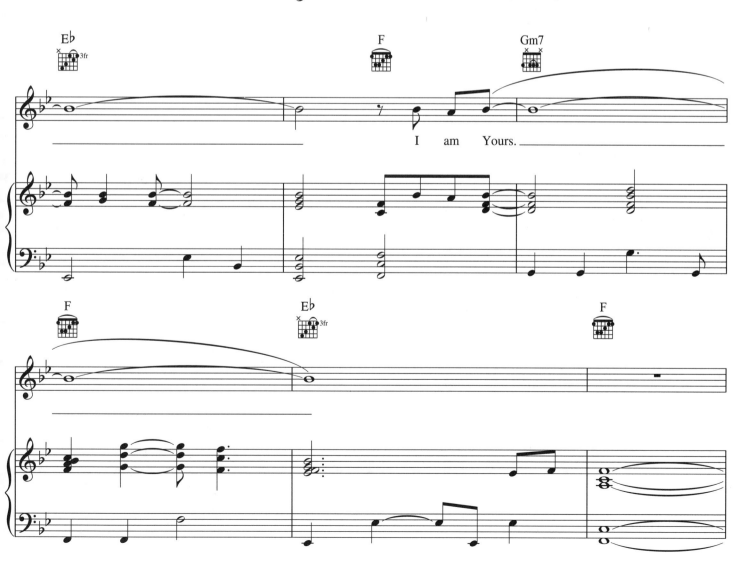

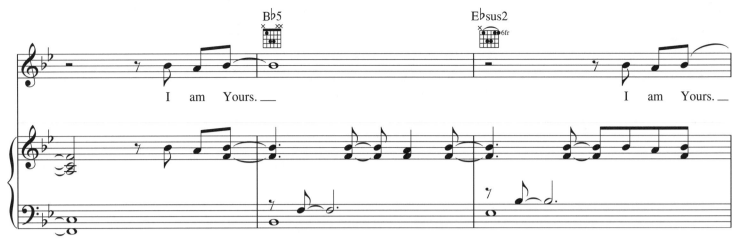

I am Yours. ___   I am Yours. ___

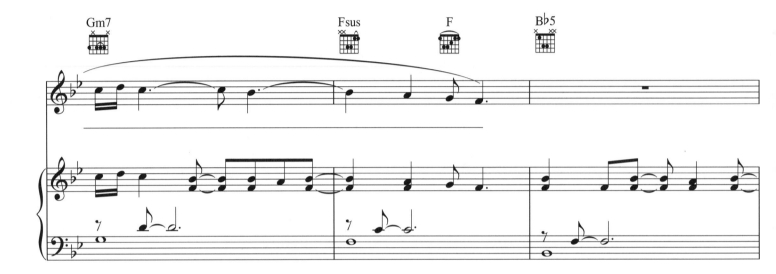

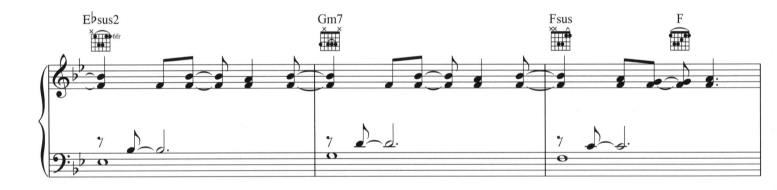

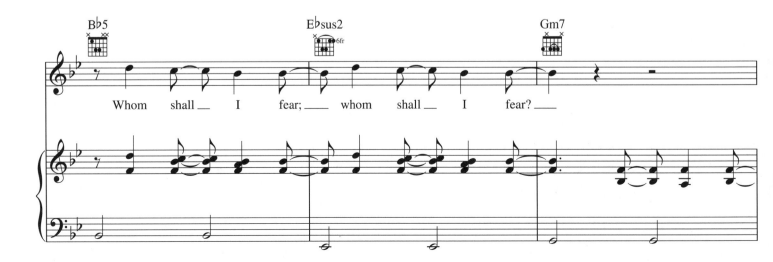

Whom shall ___ I fear; ___ whom shall ___ I fear? ___

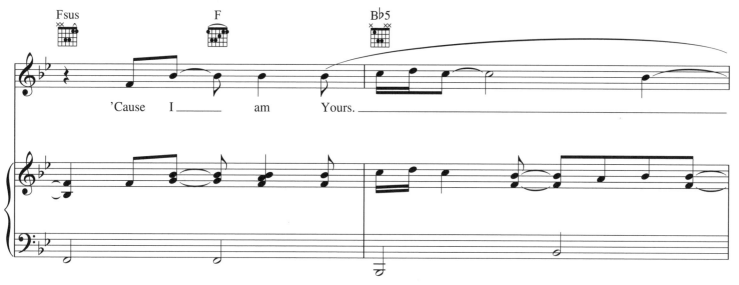

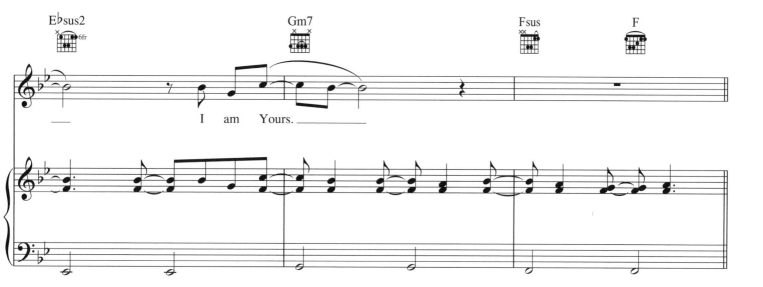

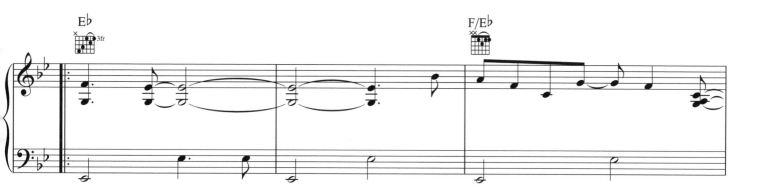

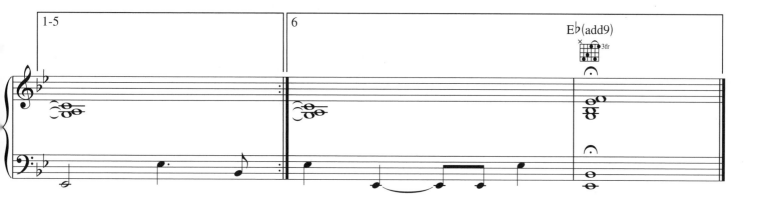

AMERICAN DREAM

Words and Music by MARK HALL
and HECTOR CERVANTES

Moderately slow

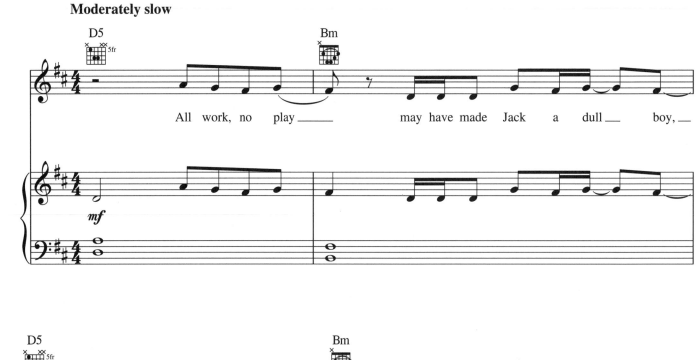

All work, no play ___ may have made Jack a dull ___ boy,

___ but all work, no God ___ has left Jack with a lost soul. ___

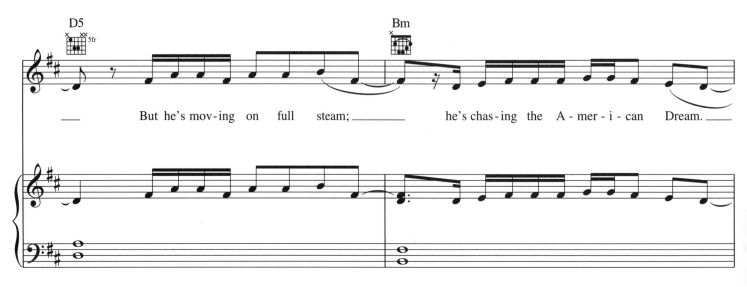

___ But he's mov-ing on full steam; ___ he's chas-ing the A-mer-i-can Dream.

He's gon - na give his fam - 'ly _____ the fin - er things. __

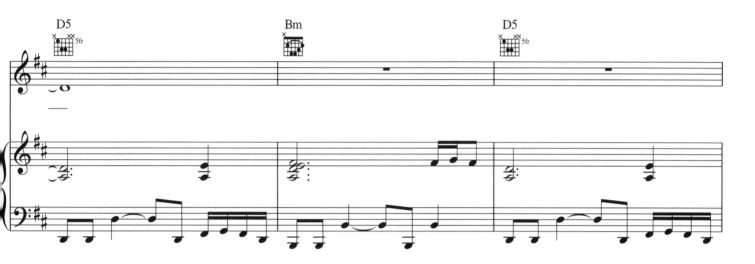

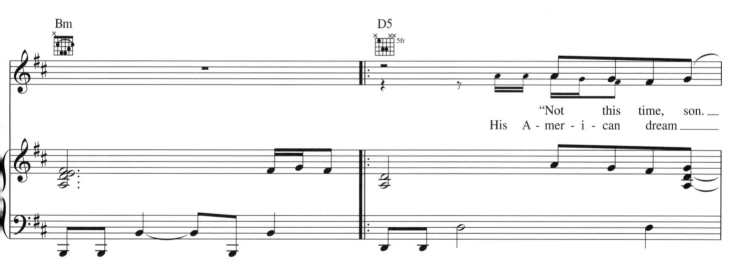

"Not this time, son. __
His A - mer - i - can dream _____

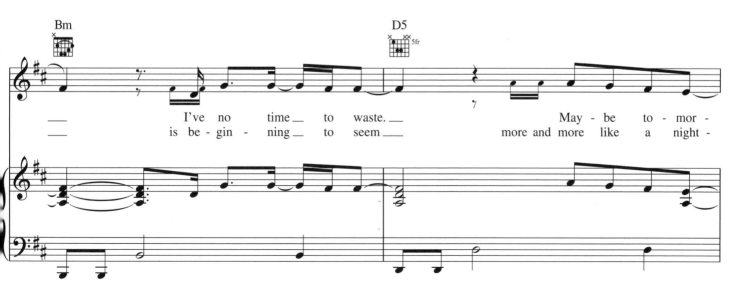

I've no time __ to waste. __ May - be to - mor -
is be - gin - ning __ to seem ___ more and more like a night -

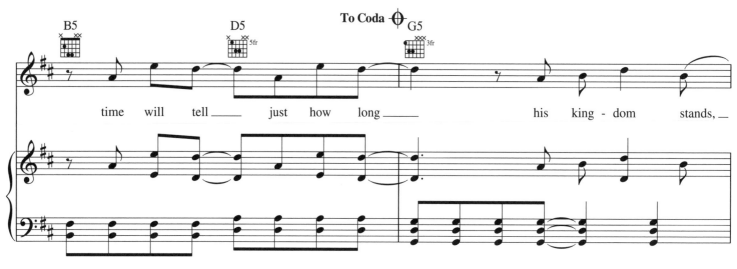

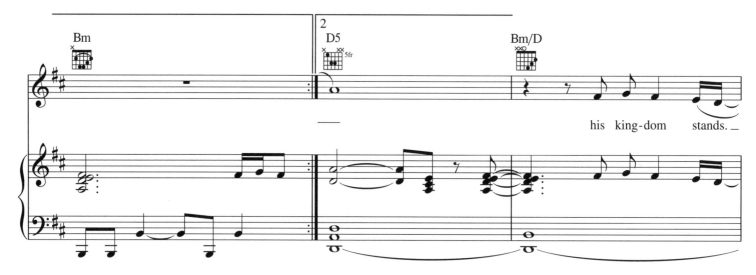

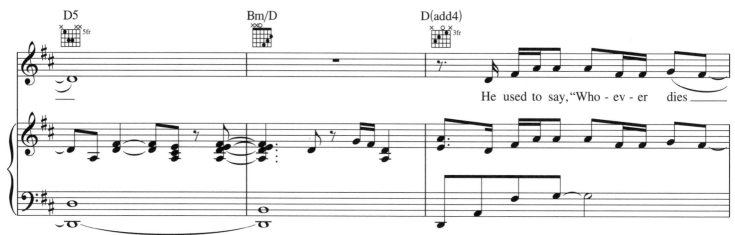

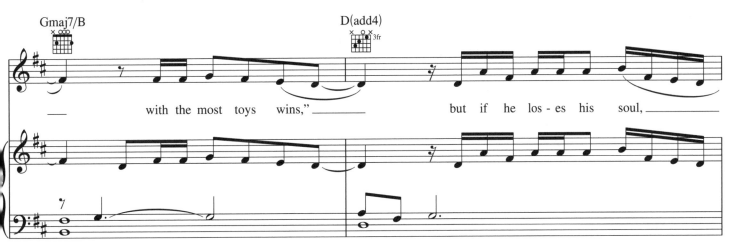

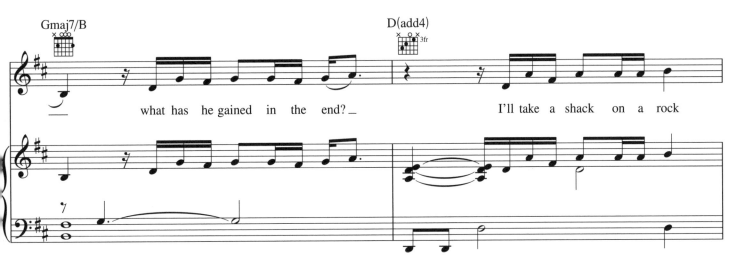

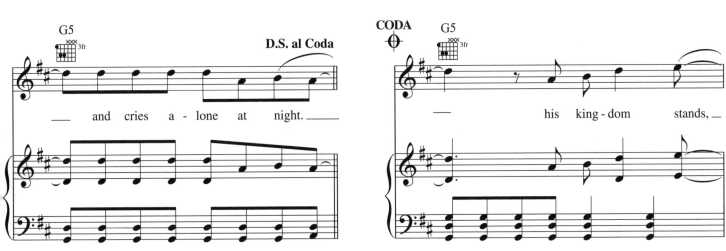

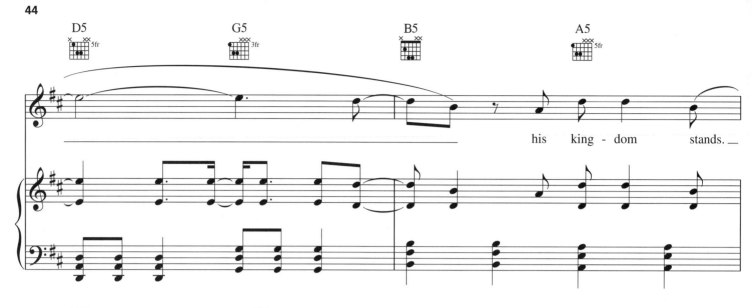

his king-dom stands.

All they real-ly want-ed was you. All they real-ly want-ed was you.

All they real-ly want-ed was you. ___

HERE I GO AGAIN

Words and Music by
MARK HALL

Moderately slow, in 1

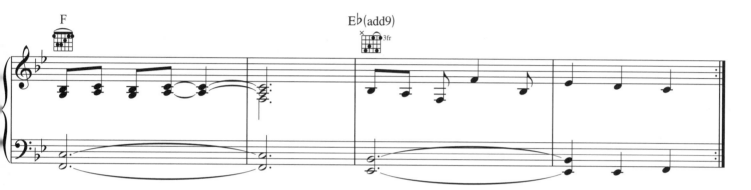

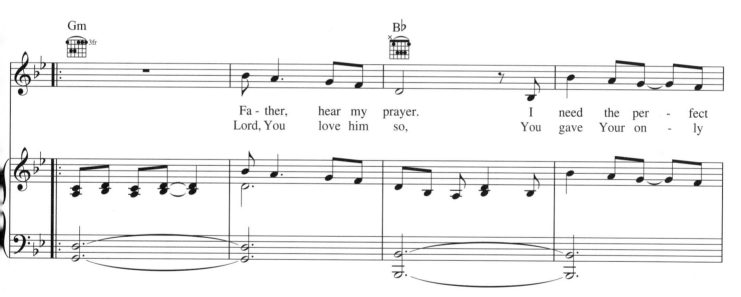

Fa - ther, hear my prayer.   I need the per - fect
Lord, You love him so,   You gave Your on - ly

words,   words that he will hear   and
Son.   If he will just be - lieve,

46

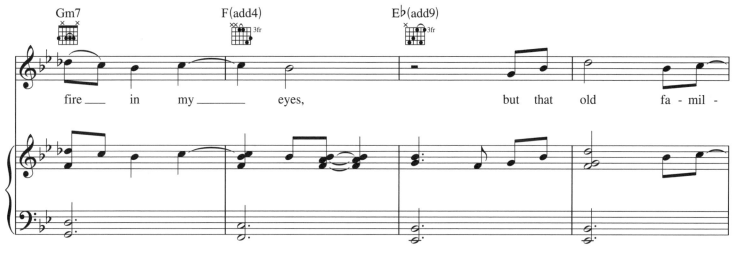

fire ___ in my _____ eyes, _____ but that old fa - mil -

- iar fear ____ is tear - ing at _____ my words. __ What am I so a -

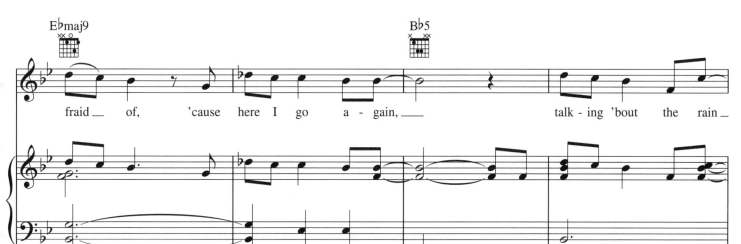

fraid ___ of, 'cause here I go a - gain, ___ talk - ing 'bout the rain __

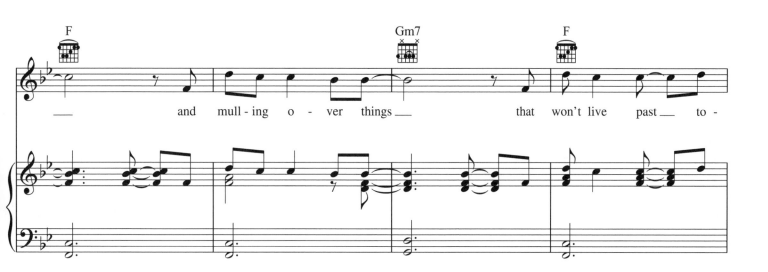

___ and mull - ing o - ver things ___ that won't live past ___ to -

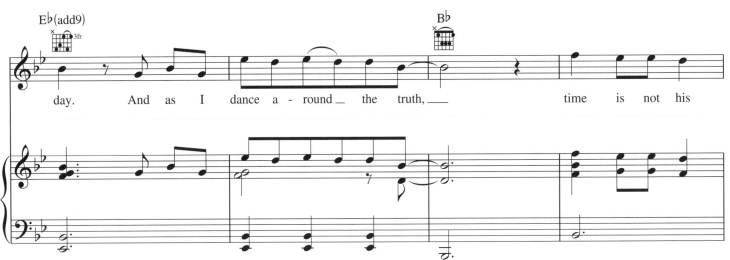

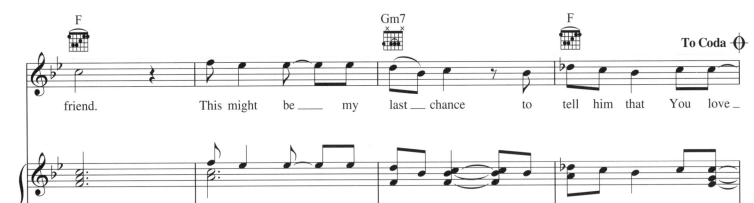

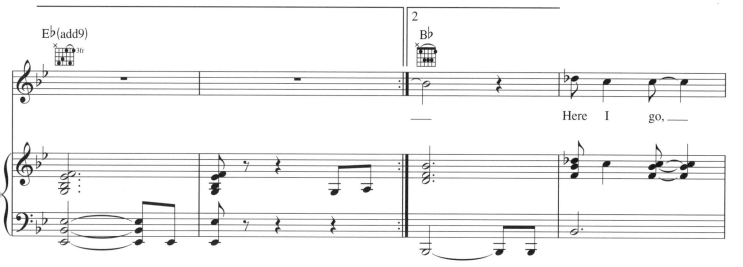

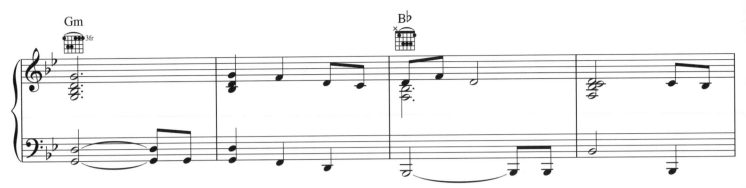

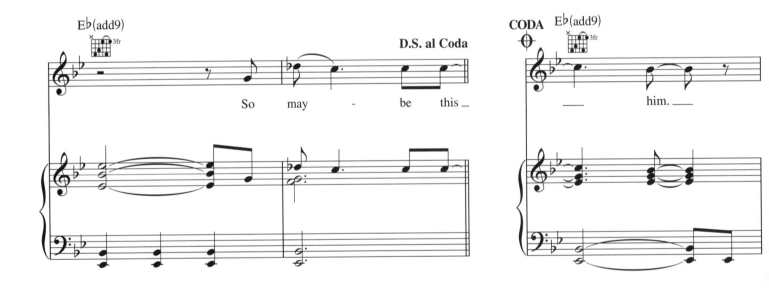

So may - be this __

him. __

This might be my last __ chance to tell him that You love __

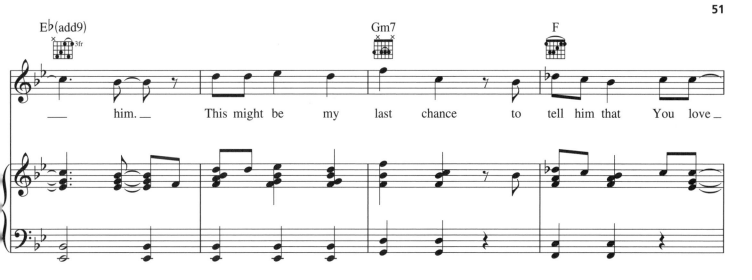

him. _ him. _ This might be my last chance to tell him that You love _

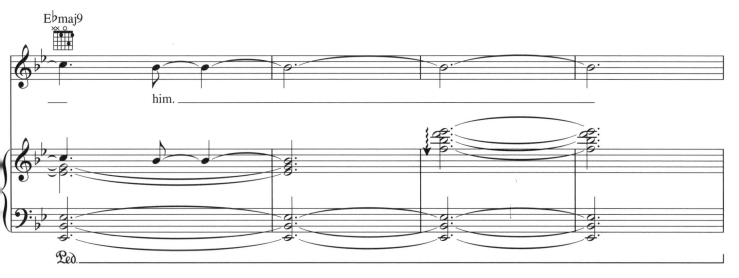

_ him. _____

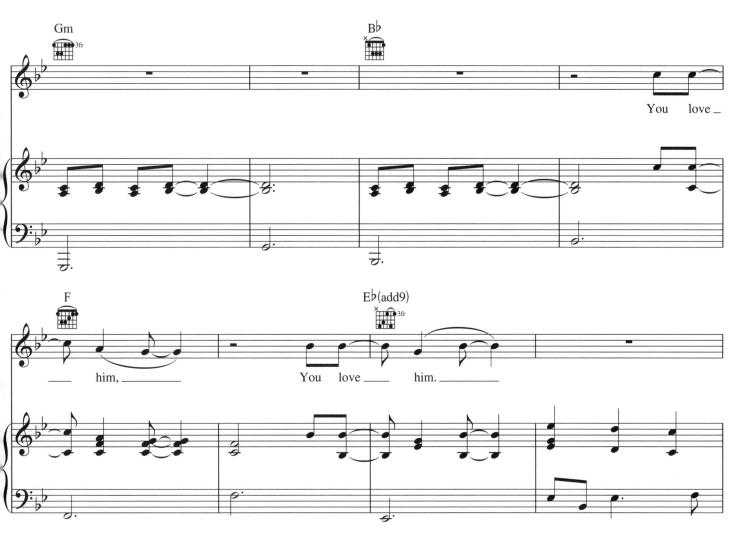

You love _

_ him, _____ You love ____ him. _____

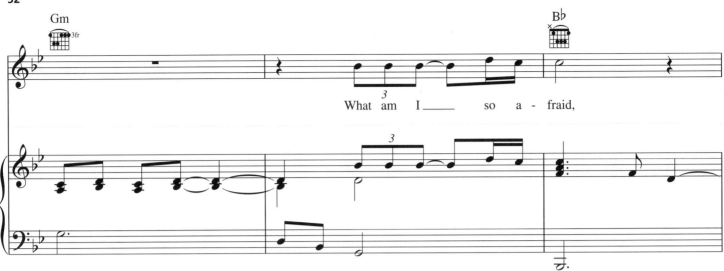

What am I___ so a-fraid,

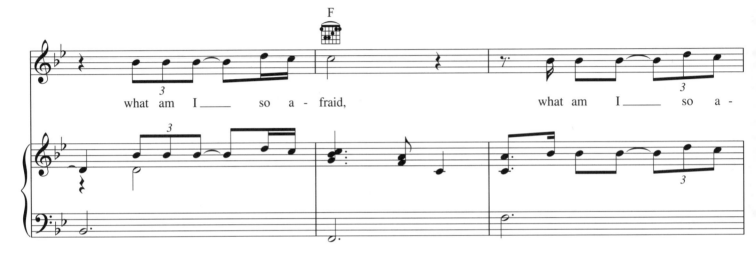

what am I___ so a-fraid,   what am I___ so a-

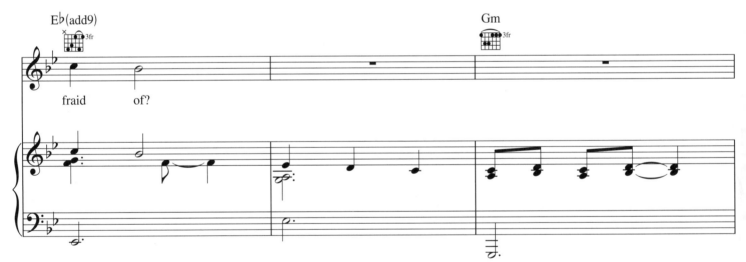

fraid of?

How, then, will he know   what he has nev-er heard?___

PRAISE YOU WITH THE DANCE

Words and Music by
MARK HALL

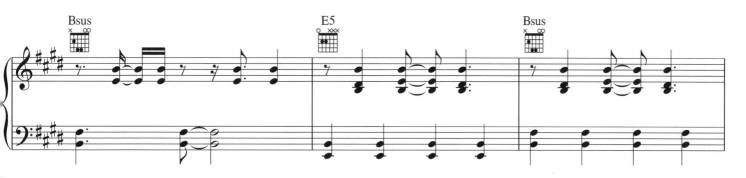

I will sing to ___ the Lord ___

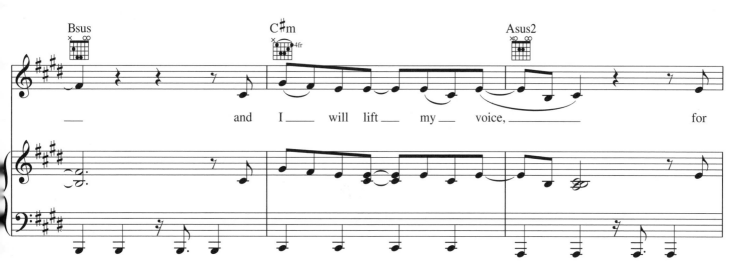

___ and I ___ will lift ___ my ___ voice, _____ for

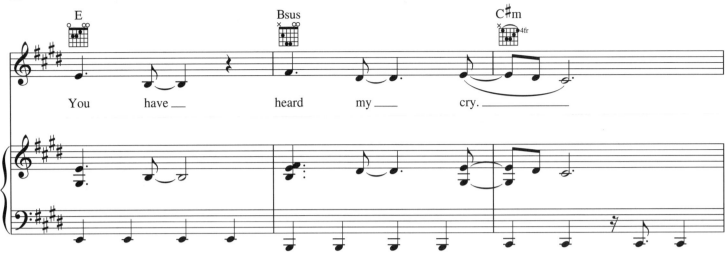

You have ___ heard my ___ cry. _____

I will sing to ___ the Lord _____ and

I will lift ___ my hands, _____ for You have ___

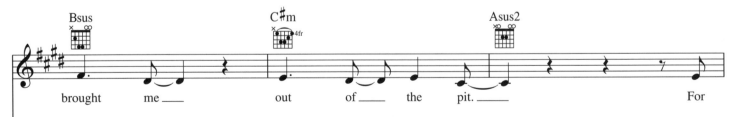

brought me ___ out of ___ the pit. _____ For

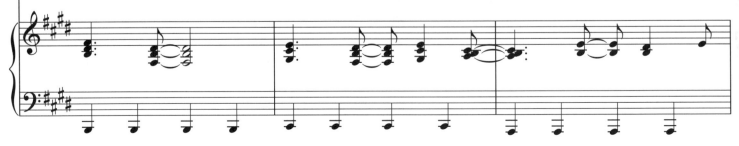

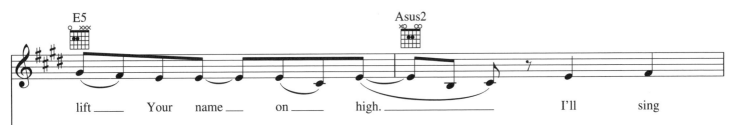

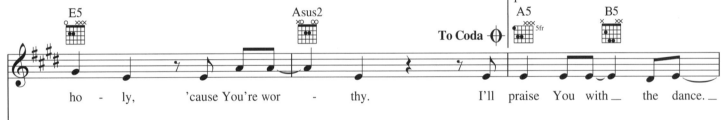

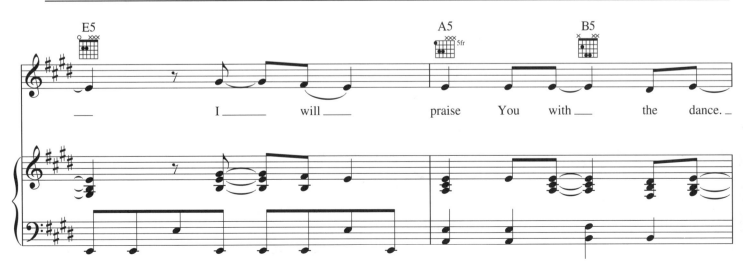

I ___ will praise You with __ the dance. ___

I will

praise You with __ the dance. ___

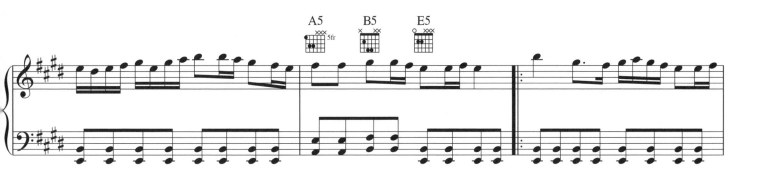

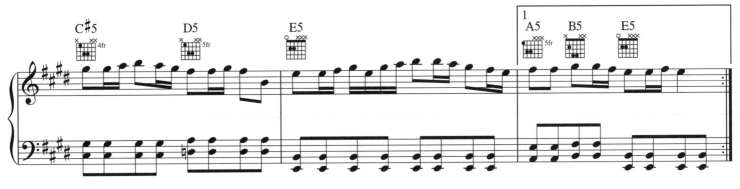

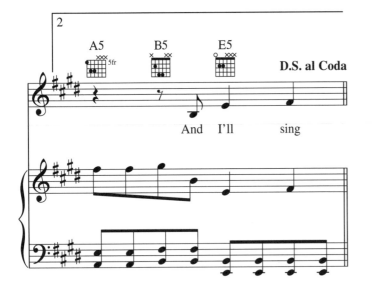

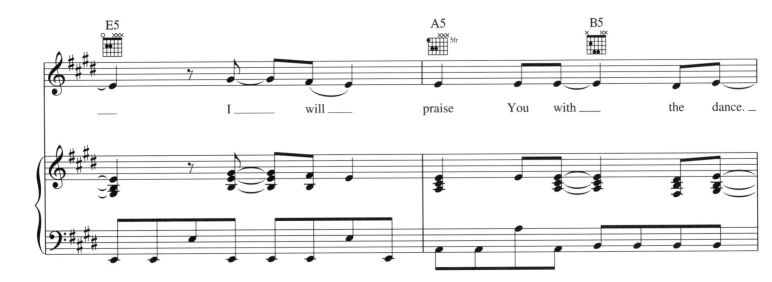

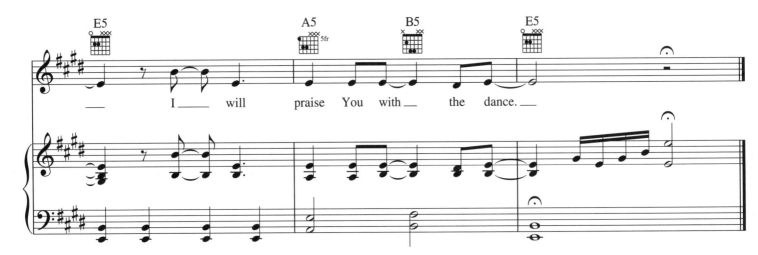

GLORY

Words and Music by MARK HALL
and HECTOR CERVANTES

Moderately fast

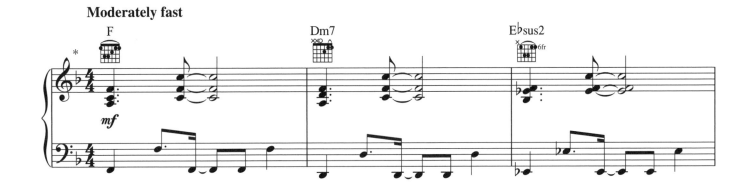

You are ho - ly in _____ this place. _____

You are wor - thy of __

* Recorded a half step higher.

my praise,__ and we wor-ship__ You.__ Je - sus,__ we

wor-ship__ You.__ You're the King of Kings__

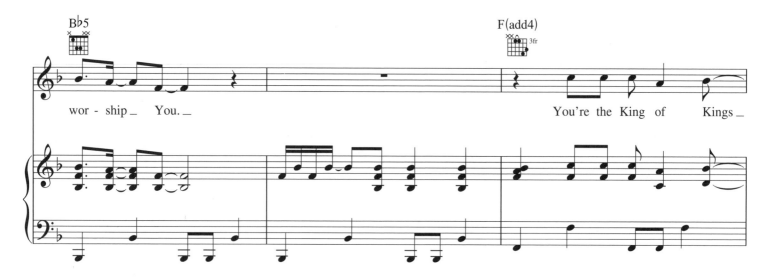

__ and the Lord__ of Lords.__ You're the Mas-ter of__ the U - ni - verse.__

__ You're the Rul-er of__ all Na-tions and we__ sing to

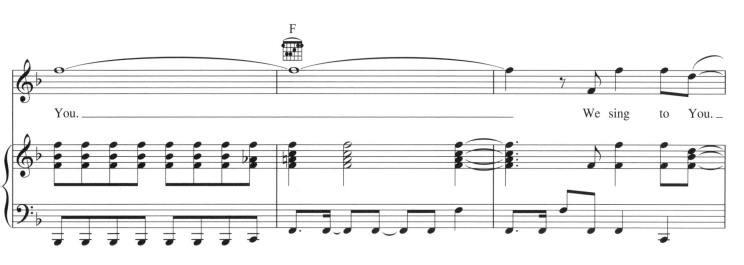

You. _____ We sing to You. _____

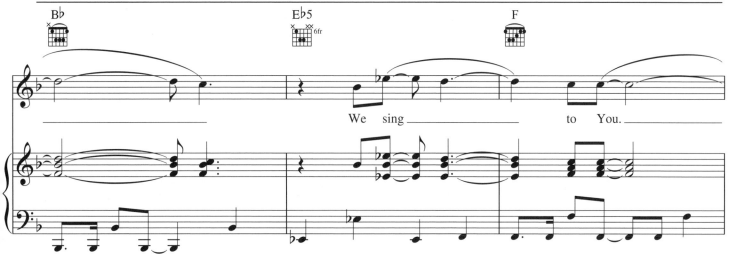

We sing _____ to You. _____

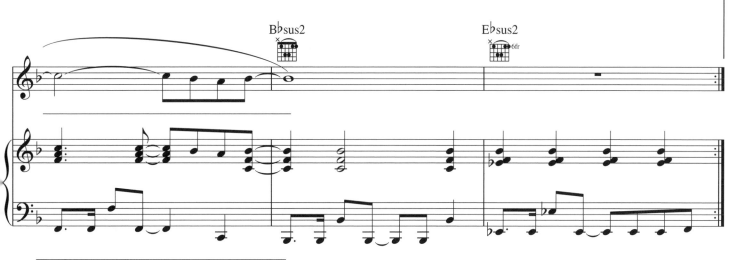

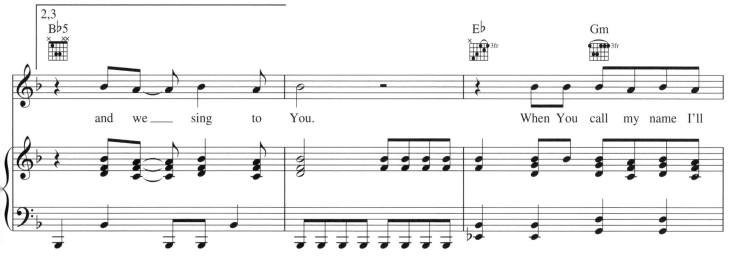

2,3

and we ___ sing to You. When You call my name I'll

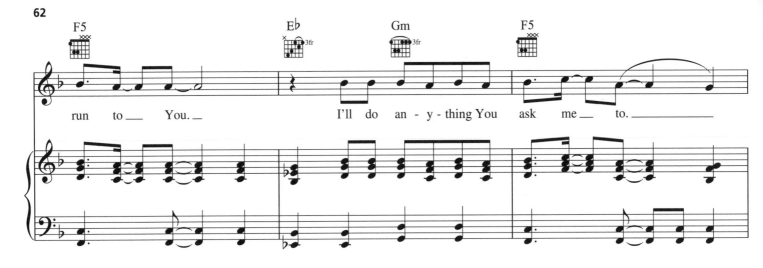

run to ___ You. ___ I'll do an - y - thing You ask me ___ to. _____

Fall - ing on my knees I'll wor - ship ___ You, ___ my Lord. _____

We give ___ You glo - ry. _____ (We give You glo - ry.) _____

___ We give ___ You glo - ry. _____ (We

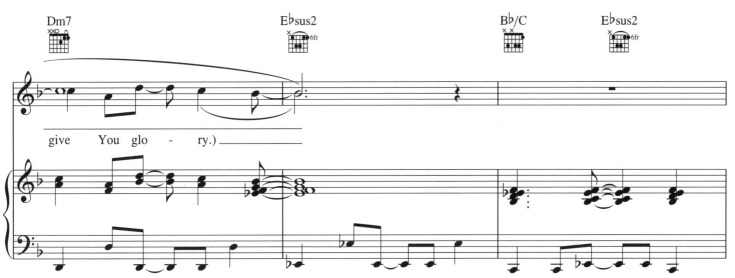

give You glo - ry.) _____

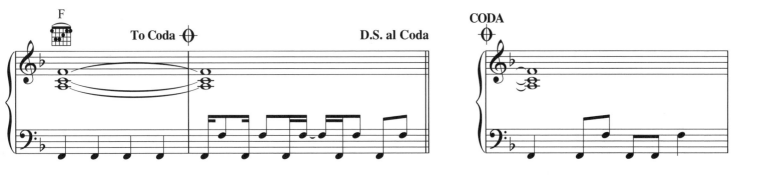

(Al - le, Al - le - lu - ia. Al - le,

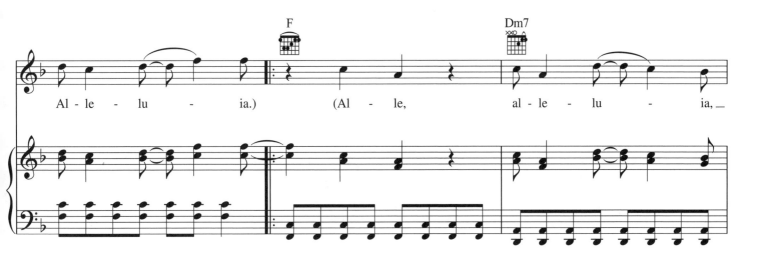

Al - le - lu - ia.) (Al - le, al - le - lu - ia, __

64

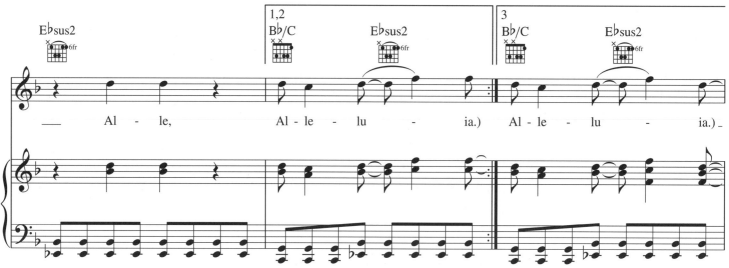

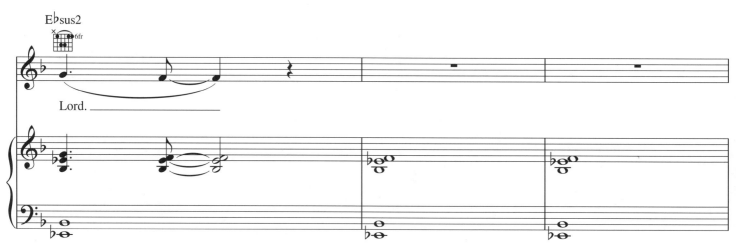

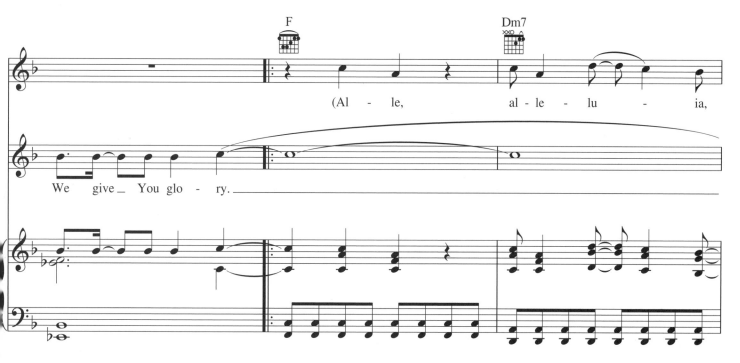

(Al - le, al - le - lu - ia,

We give _ You glo - ry. _____

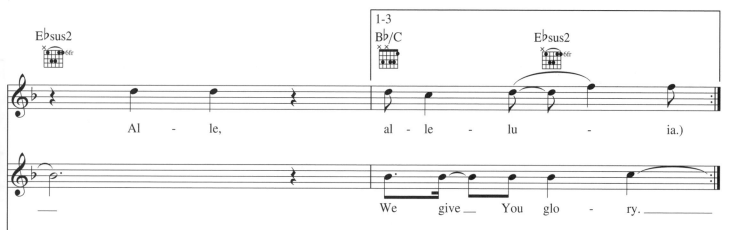

Al - le, al - le - lu - ia.)

We give _ You glo - ry. _____

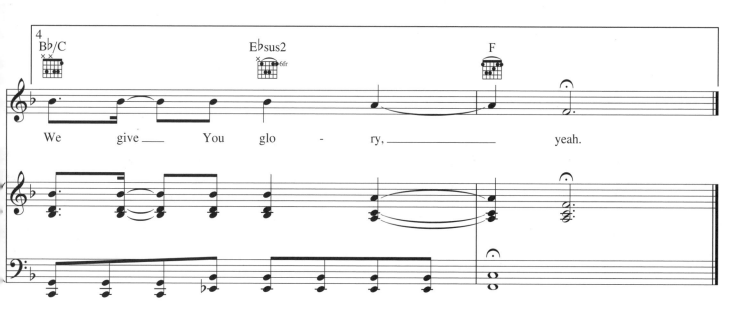

We give ___ You glo - ry, _____ yeah.

LIFE OF PRAISE

Words and Music by
MARK HALL

so much __ more. __ *Male:* For You __

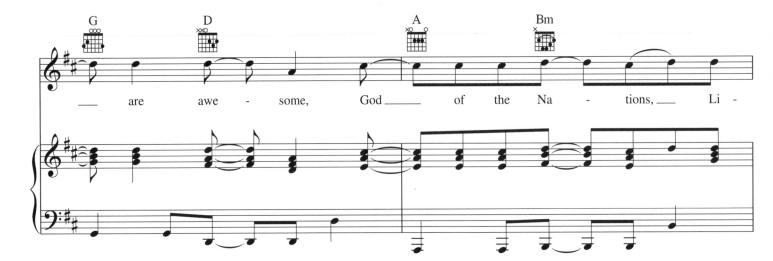

__ are awe - some, God __ of the Na - tions, __ Li -

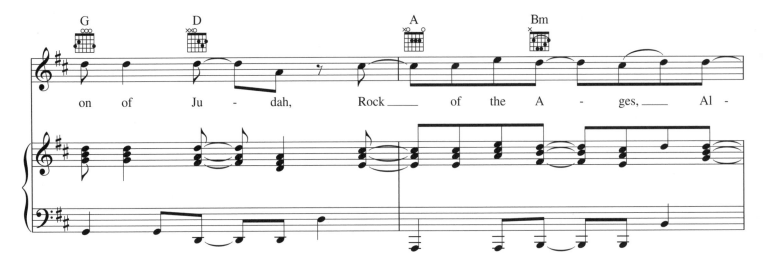

on of Ju - dah, Rock __ of the A - ges, __ Al -

- pha, O - me - ga, You're wor - thy of __ all praise. __

More than _____ these hands _____ I'll raise, _____

I'll live _____ a life _____ of praise, _____

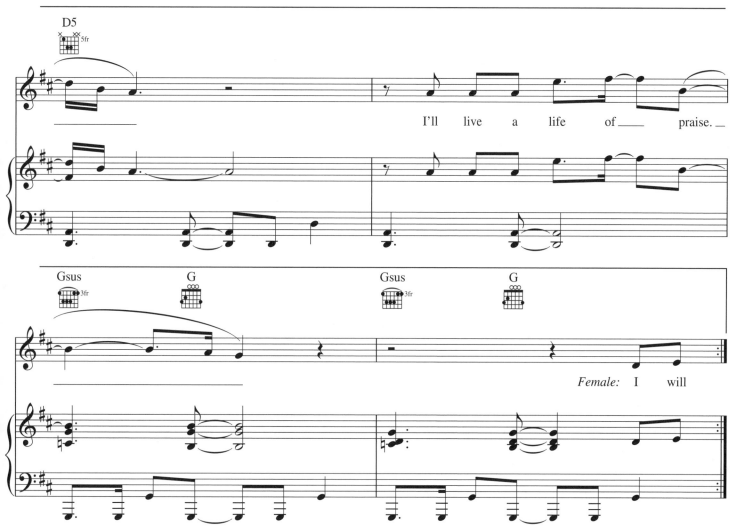

I'll live a life of _____ praise. _____

Female: I will

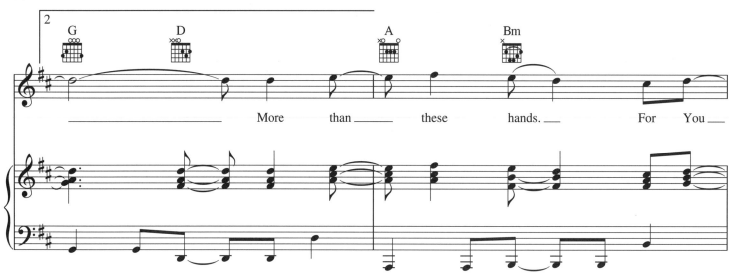

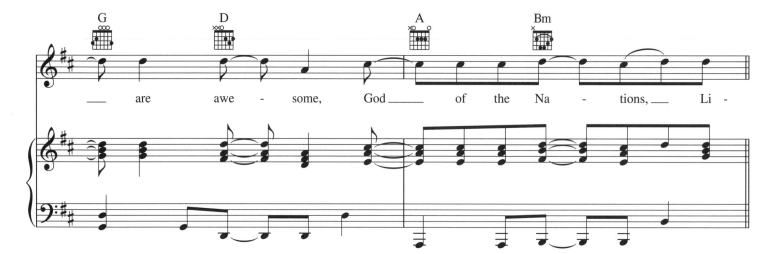

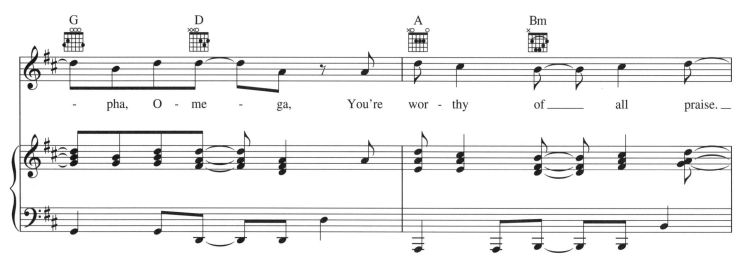

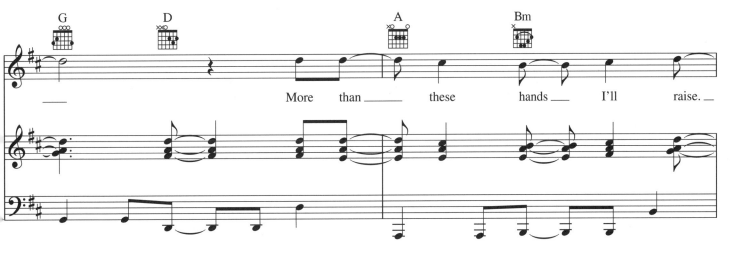

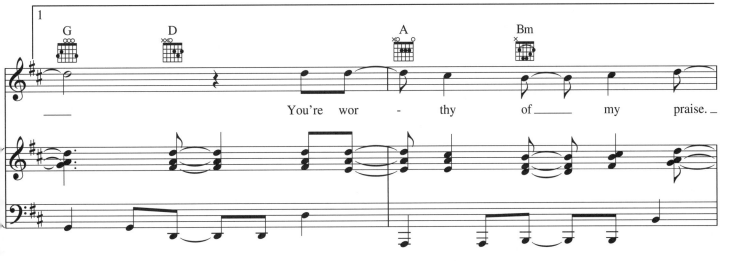

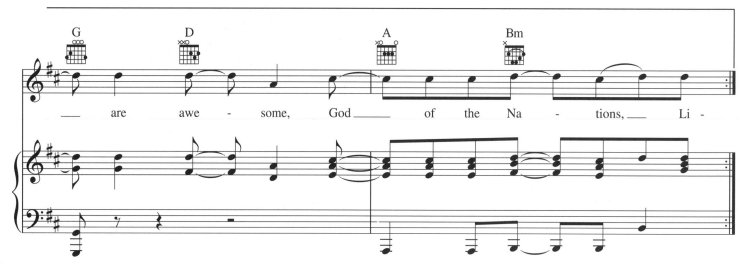

are awe - some, God ____ of the Na - tions, ___ Li -

___ You're wor - thy of ____ my ___ praise. ___
Female: (You ___

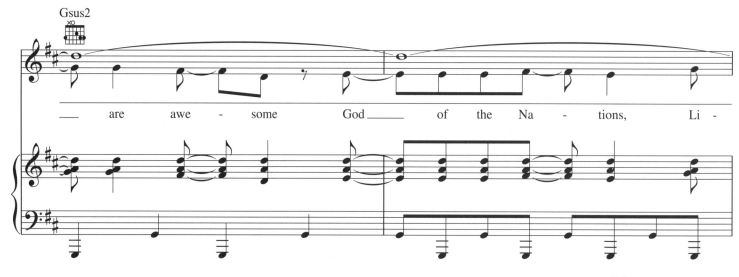

___ are awe - some God ____ of the Na - tions, ___ Li -

on of Ju - dah, Rock ____ of the A - ges.)

YOUR LOVE IS EXTRAVAGANT

Words and Music by
DARRELL EVANS

Moderately slow

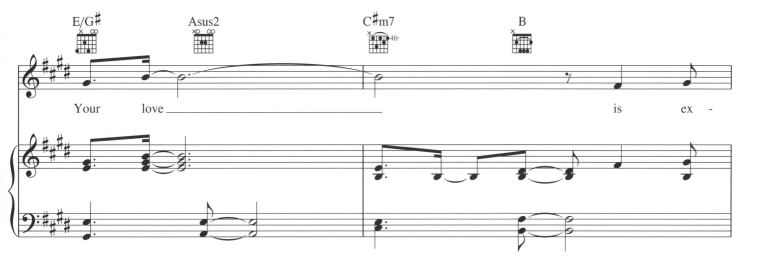

Your love _____ is ex-

trav-a-gant. ___ Your

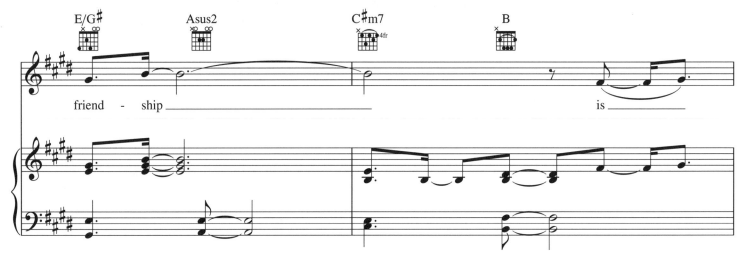

friend - ship _____ is _____

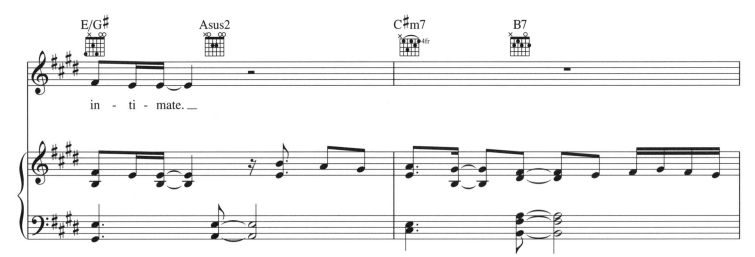

in - ti - mate. __

I feel __ like mov - ing to the rhy-thm of Your grace. __ Your frag - rance

is in - tox - i - cat - ing in a se - cret __ place, __ { 'cause and }

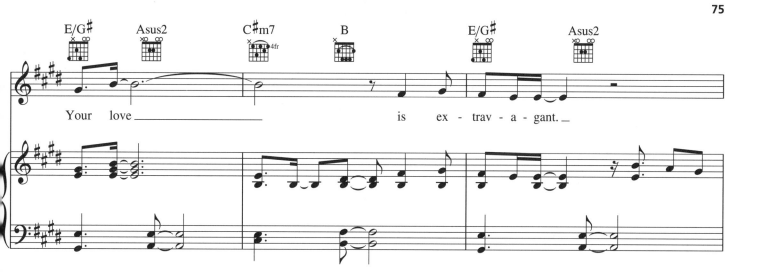

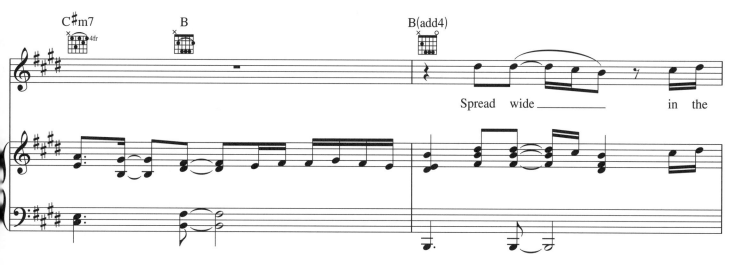

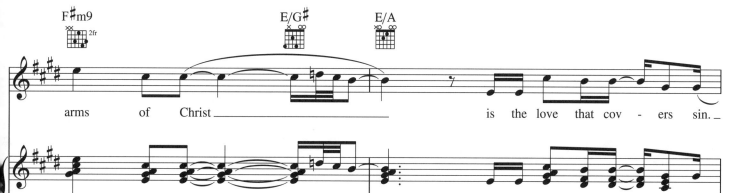

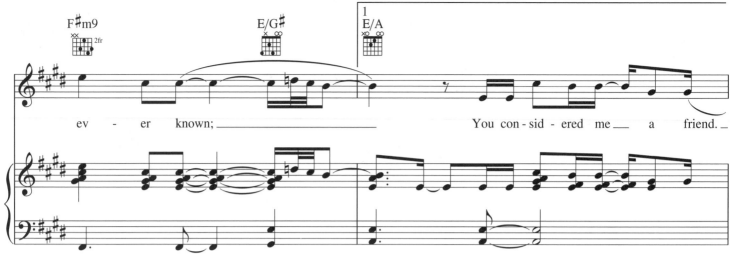

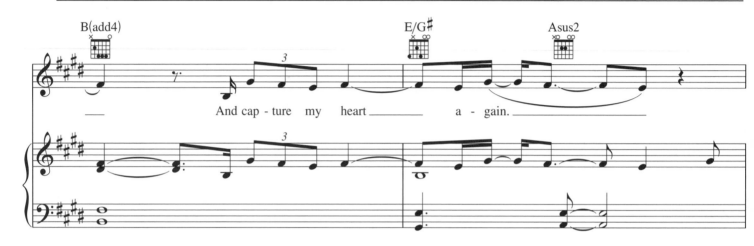

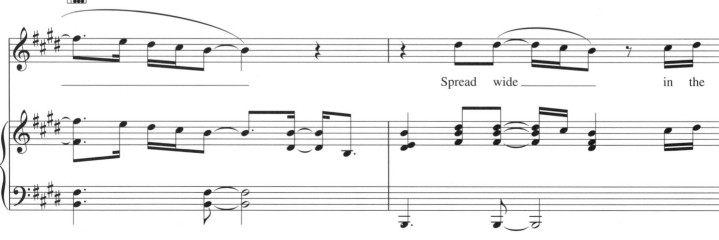

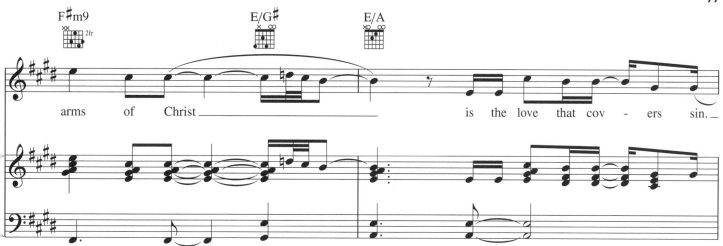

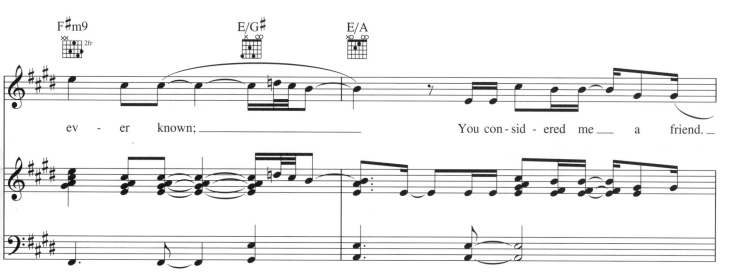

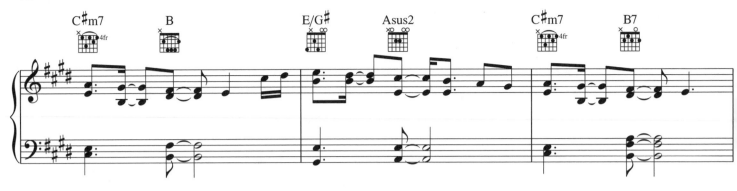

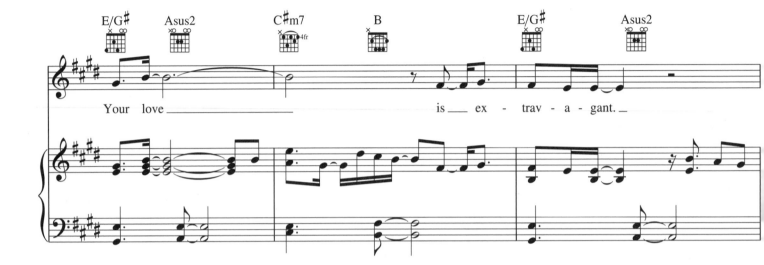

Your love _____ is ex - trav - a - gant. ___

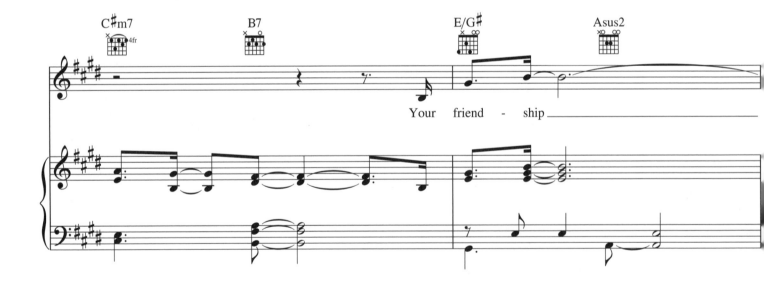

Your friend - ship _____

___ is _____ in - ti - mate. ___

More Contemporary Christian Folios from Hal Leonard

THE VERY BEST OF AVALON – TESTIFY TO LOVE

Our matching folio features all 16 songs from the 2003 compilation by this acclaimed CCM vocal quartet: Adonai • Always Have, Always Will • Can't Live a Day • Don't Save It All for Christmas Day • Everything to Me • Give It Up • The Glory (Of the Blood) • The Greatest Story • I Don't Want to Go • In Not Of • Knockin' on Heaven's Door • New Day • Pray • Take You at Your Word • Testify to Love • Wonder Why.

_____ 00306526 Piano/Vocal/Guitar $16.95

STEVEN CURTIS CHAPMAN – DECLARATION

13 songs: Bring It On • Carry You to Jesus • Declaration of Dependence • God Follower • God Is God • Jesus Is Life • Live Out Loud • Magnificent Obsession • No Greater Love • Savior • See the Glory • This Day • When Love Takes You In.

_____ 00306453 Piano/Vocal/Guitar $14.95

DC TALK – INTERMISSION: THE GREATEST HITS

17 of DC Talk's best: Between You and Me • Chance • Colored People • Consume Me • Hardway (Remix) • I Wish We'd All Been Ready • In the Light • Jesus Freak • Jesus Is Just Alright • Luv Is a Verb • Mind's Eye • My Will • Say the Words (Now) • Socially Acceptable • SugarCoat It • Supernatural • What If I Stumble.

_____ 00306414 Piano/Vocal/Guitar $14.95

JEFF DEYO – SATURATE

Features 14 powerful tracks, including: All I Want • I Give You My Heart • I'd Rather Have Jesus • Let It Flow • Let Me Burn • Lose Myself • Many Crowns • More Love, More Power • Satisfy • Sing to You • Thank You for Life • You Are Good • You Are Good (Piano & Cello Movement) • You Are Good (Orchestral Movement).

_____ 00306484 Piano/Vocal/Guitar $14.95

KEITH GREEN – THE ULTIMATE COLLECTION

Our 20-song collection matches Sparrow's latest compilation CD of the late, great Keith Green, who died in a plane crash in 1982. Includes: Asleep in the Light • I Can't Believe It • I Want to Be More like Jesus • Jesus Commands Us to Go • Make My Life a Prayer to You • My Eyes Are Dry • Oh Lord, You're Beautiful • Pledge My Head to Heaven • Rushing Wind • Soften Your Heart • There Is a Redeemer • You Are the One • You! • Your Love Broke Through • and more.

_____ 00306518 Piano/Vocal/Guitar $16.95

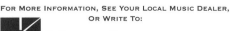

JENNIFER KNAPP – THE WAY I AM

Includes all 12 tunes from the critically acclaimed CD: Around Me • Breathe on Me • By and By • Charity • Come to Me • Fall Down • In Two (The Lament) • Light of the World • No Regrets • Say Won't You Say • Sing Mary Sing • The Way I Am.

_____ 00306467 Piano/Vocal/Guitar $14.95

THE MARTINS – GLORIFY/EDIFY/TESTIFY

Features 16 songs: Be Thou My Vision • Gentle Shepherd • Healer of My Heart • In Christ Alone • Jesus, I Am Resting • Lord Most High • Pass Me Not • Redeemed • Settle on My Soul • So High • You Are Holy • more. Includes vocal harmony parts.

_____ 00306492 Piano/Vocal/Guitar $14.95

NICHOLE NORDEMAN – WOVEN & SPUN

Includes all 11 songs from the 2002 release of this Dove Award nominee: Doxology • Even Then • Gratitude • Healed • Holy • I Am • Legacy • Mercies New • My Offering • Never Loved You More • Take Me As I Am.

_____ 00306494 Piano/Vocal/Guitar $14.95

SMOKIE NORFUL – I NEED YOU NOW

The son of a Chicago pastor, funky R&B/soul/gospel artist Smokie Norful has made a name for himself with his wonderful voice. Our songbook includes all 10 tracks from his critically acclaimed debut: I Need You Now • It's All About You • Just Can't Stop • The Least I Can Do • Life's Not Promised • Praise Him • Psalm 64 • Same Sad Song • Somethin', Somethin' • Still Say, Thank You.

_____ 00306554 Piano/Vocal/Guitar $14.95

STACIE ORRICO

All 12 genre-crossing songs from the eponymous sophomore album from 17-year-old Stacie Orrico, who the All Music Guide calls "America's newest diva/role model." Includes: Bounce Back • Hesitation • I Could Be the One • I Promise • Instead • Maybe I Won't Look Back • (There's Gotta Be) More to Life • Security • Strong Enough • Stuck • That's What Love's About • Tight.

_____ 00306548 Piano/Vocal/Guitar $14.95

THE BEST OF OUT OF EDEN

A great compilation of 13 hit songs: Come and Take My Hand • A Friend • Get to Heaven • Greater Love • If You Really Knew Me • Lookin' for Love • More Than You Know • River • Show Me • There Is a Love • and more.

_____ 00306381 Piano/Vocal/Guitar $14.95

TWILA PARIS – GREATEST HITS

This folio celebrates Twila's career with 18 hits: Destiny • Faithful Friend • God Is in Control • He Is Exalted • How Beautiful • Lamb of God • Run to You • The Time Is Now • We Bow Down • We Will Glorify • and more.

_____ 00306449 Piano/Vocal/Guitar $14.95

PHILLIPS, CRAIG AND DEAN – LET YOUR GLORY FALL

Our matching folio features all ten inspirational tunes from this popular CCM trio's 2003 release: Every Day • Fall Down • Hallelujah (Your Love Is Amazing) • Here I Am to Worship • How Deep the Father's Love for Us • Lord, Let Your Glory Fall • My Praise • Only You • What Kind of Love Is This • The Wonderful Cross.

_____ 00306519 Piano/Vocal/Guitar $14.95

MATT REDMAN – THE FATHER'S SONG

Features 14 songs: The Father's Song • Holy Moment • Justice and Mercy • King of This Heart • Let My Words Be Few • Light of the World • Nothing Is Too Much • O Sacred King • Revelation • Take the World but Give Me Jesus • You Must Increase • more.

_____ 00306378 Piano/Vocal/Guitar $14.95

REBECCA ST. JAMES – WORSHIP GOD

Includes 12 worship tunes: Above All • Better Is One Day • Breathe • God of Wonders • It Is Well with My Soul • Lamb of God • Let My Words Be Few • More Than the Watchmen • Omega (Remix) • Quiet You with My Love • Song of Love • You.

_____ 00306473 Piano/Vocal/Guitar $14.95

THIRD DAY – OFFERINGS II ALL I HAVE TO GIVE

14 songs from the chart-topping 2003 release by this popular Christian band with a Southern rock sound. Includes: Anything • Creed • The Everlasting • Give • God of Wonders • May Your Wonders Never Cease • Nothing Compares • Offering • Show Me Your Glory • Sing a Song • Take My Life • Turn Your Eyes upon Jesus • You Are So Good to Me • Your Love Oh Lord.

_____ 00306541 Piano/Vocal/Guitar $14.95

ZOEGIRL

11 terrific songs from this debut album: Anything Is Possible • Constantly • Give Me One Reason • I Believe • Little Did I Know • Live Life • Living for You • No You • Stop Right There • Suddenly • Upside Down.

_____ 00306455 Piano/Vocal/Guitar $14.95